A

LETTER

TO

J. H. WILKINS, H. B. ROGERS, AND F. B. FAY,

COMMISSIONERS OF MASSACHUSETTS

FOR THE

STATE REFORM SCHOOL FOR GIRLS.

BY

S. G. HOWE.

BOSTON:
TICKNOR AND FIELDS.
MDCCCLIV.

THURSTON AND TORRY, PRINTERS.

LETTER.

Boston, Nov. 10, 1854.

Messrs. John H. Wilkins, Henry B. Rogers, Francis B. Fay,
Commissioners appointed by the Governor of Massachusetts to select and determine the location, and prepare plans and estimates of the building for a State Reform School for Girls, with a system for its organization and government, &c. &c.

Gentlemen, — I thank you for the circular of the 3d instant, which you were pleased to send me.

In 1850, a letter upon the same subject was received from the Hon. William Appleton, to which I replied at length. The reply has not been printed; and as it contains some views which you may possibly think worth considering, though they are not common or popular, and as I am not able to answer your thirty questions so fully as their importance demands, I send it to you for want of a better. My great interest in the subject, however, will not permit me to lose this opportunity for the expression of some thoughts suggested by your Circular, and of some criticisms, the freedom of which your liberality will pardon.

I am glad to see that the sacred social duty of attempting to reform vicious or viciously disposed girls is at last to be undertaken by the State. But I am sorry to see, as I do, in the spirit of the Resolutions of the Legislature, and in the tenor of your questions, that this delicate and difficult task is to be attempted by the machinery of an establishment similar to the great Reform School for Boys at Westborough.

There is an instinctive shudder at the thought of bringing together, under one roof, or into one establishment, two or three hundred unchaste or unchastely disposed girls; and reflection shows that the instinct is a true one.

Such an establishment would be wrong in principle, because it would be upon the plan of *congregation* and *approximation* of vicious material; whereas the true principle requires its *separation* and *diffusion.**

Such an establishment would be almost necessarily wrong in its administration, because it would require such physical restraint and coercion, as are most undesirable and dangerous instruments in establishments for moral reform, especially those for the reformation of girls.

I think that an instinctive perception of the difficulties of the case, and of the inapplicability of the common plan of treatment, has hitherto prevented public action in behalf of these unfortunate and perishing creatures. Benevolent men and women have thought earnestly upon the subject, and urged it upon the Legislature. Wise and good men have there given it their attention for a while, but sorrowfully dismissed it, in view of the difficulties which surround it. At last the presure has become so strong that something must be done. The plan contemplated by the Legislature, and by you also, — as is indicated by the tenor of your questions, — is the one which most readily suggests itself, because it seems the simplest and cheapest, and is commonly adopted in the discharge of what are called public charities.

Let us see, however, whether it is necessary to adopt this plan; and in order to do so, let us consider, as impartially as we can, the principles and the administration of our public charitable institutions generally.

I admit the great merits of those establishments, especially of such as are independent of political influences. I admit their excellence. But then excellence is only comparative. We may excel others, but still be far behind the greatest attainable perfection.

The public institutions of a country grow out of the public wants. They are generally true indications of the public enlightenment and sense of duty. The heart and sentiment of the people are sure to be just; but more culture and knowledge than they generally get is needed to guide them aright.

* This matter is enlarged upon in the letter to Mr. Appleton.

Public institutions are of various kinds, some having embodiment in buildings, others, though very important ones, working without visible machinery.

Light-houses, custom-houses, court-houses, and the like, are in one sense, public institutions; they are as much the offspring of a sense of public duty as alms-houses, hospitals, or orphan asylums are; and the esteem in which they are held, and the mode in which they are administered, indicate the state of the public heart and conscience. We may even consider banks, manufactories and the like, as public institutions, though not under the management of the agents of the whole people.

Now if one should ask why an orphan asylum should be called a public *charitable* institution any more than a light-house should be so called, the question would be a very unsatisfactory one to most people, but the answer would be more unsatisfactory to the few who would seek it.

There are certain public institutions which seem immediately to concern the public thrift and the public Safety, as light-houses, manufactories, and the like, — others which concern the public Charity and Beneficence. Now are these considered as of equal importance, and regarded with equal interest? I trow not. The first are sure to be built upon the best plan, and conducted with great skill; but it is not always so with the others.

Commissioners for building a light-house would never advertise for *bids* from the towns along shore for the privilege of having the edifice in their borders, but Commissioners for public charitable institutions are wont to do so. The light-house is sure to go upon the very best spot, cost what it may; the public charitable institution is likely to go upon the cheapest.

We have, just now, a case which so strongly shows the folly of this policy, that you will excuse its mention.

The Commissioners, appointed by the Governor of Massachusetts, to select and determine a spot for the new Hospital for the Insane, were lured, by certain apparent pecuniary advantages to the State, into accepting as a gift a certain tract of land in the town of Taunton, which was a very unsuitable one. To say nothing of other serious objections, the lack of an abundance of fresh water is a fatal one.

A Hospital for the Insane should be placed where there is a

ceaseless flow of sweet water from a fountain-head that will carry it over the ridge-pole. Not only should there be no stint, no necessity for pumping, no reliance upon machinery, but there should be an abundance, and more even than enough. We should no more go to calculating how many gallons will be needed for daily supply, than we should calculate how many cubic feet of atmosphere there ought to be overhead. We should make sure of more than enough for all possible uses, and then for the luxury of having it 'run to waste,' as is said. But there is no waste in nature. Running water is beautiful, and therefore useful. It should gush up and flow over, and run freely through the grounds of a hospital, to gladden the eye, and make music for the ear, and be an ever sporting, sparkling 'thing of life.' Now this might have been procured, because the Commissioners had full power, and whole counties to range over; but they pitched upon a rough 'pine barren,' where there is not an inch of soil to make a garden, and where there was only a *single well* to supply water. From this the water was to be toilfully drawn and forced up into the house. The hospital was no sooner in operation, than it was on short allowance of water; and the present Trustees are laying pipes to a neighboring mill-pond. With a strainer to keep out the tadpoles, and a steam-engine, they will do all that can be done, to remedy the penny-wise and pound-foolish blunder of the Commissioners. But 'all that can be done' is comparatively little; for, to say nothing of depending for a supply of water upon the machinery of a steam-engine, and the watchfulness of an engineer, the fluid, when obtained, can never be in that condition which is best suited for man's drink.

Water should be drank when sparkling freshly from the earth; but this is water that sprang to life in far-off fountains, trickled in rills, ran in brooks, flowed faintly in a river, rested in a pond, and now, having nearly finished its course in the great circuit, having nearly lived out its life, is about to be buried in the great tomb of all waters, to await a new birth.

Water, like every thing organized, has its youth and its age; and the patients of the hospital at Taunton must always drink *old water*, yea, even old Taunton river water, which is proverbially weak, and all because the Commissioners, anxious to make a good bargain for the State, listened to the bid of Taunton folks, as the most advantageous one, and located the hospital there. Or rather, if the evil be traced to its source, because the Governor thought it was good policy for him to select one Commissioner from each of the three great political parties.

I have alluded to this error of the Commissioners, not because it is the only one, but because it struck me most forcibly. That my objections to much of what they did, are not merely theoretical, is proved by the fact, that as soon as the building was finished, and delivered by the Commissioners to the Trustees and Superintendents who were to manage it, they immediately proceeded to demolish certain parts of the work, and to alter others.

To be a 'know nothing' in politics may be, just now, the best qualification for political office; but surely it is settled that to be a know nothing in matters pertaining to the insane, is not the best qualification for Commissioner for selecting sites and building hospitals.

If a Governor of Massachusetts, in his capacity of President of a manufacturing company, should have to appoint three Commissioners for selecting a site and building a factory to be run by water, he would diligently seek men fully acquainted with the manufacturing business, even if they should be all of one political party. And if any town should offer to *give* a lot of land, and ten thousand dollars into the bargain, provided the said Commissioners would build the factory upon it, they would not even consider the offer, unless there was a good waterfall at hand; certainly not if they were stockholders in the company.

Now manufactories are, as I have said, in one sense, public institutions. None but an able and skilful man would be thought of to build and organize one of them, belong he to what party he might, and have he ever so many prefixes to his name; while almost any body will do to build and organize a hospital, provided he belongs to a particular party, be an *honorable*, and want the appointment. The first is paid the very highest wages, and is cheap at that; the second is paid the very lowest, or nothing at all, and is dear even at that.

It is well known to those familiar with the subject, that in almost every instance in the United States where a Hospital for the Insane has been turned over by the Building Commissioners to the Trustees and Superintendent, these latter have had to go to work, as the Trustees are now working at Taunton, and do all that they can to remedy the blunders of 'their illustrious predecessors.'

Do not these things show, that in the organization of Institutions in which public thrift and safety are concerned, more ability, skill and care are exercised, than in those where public beneficence and charity are to be administered?

There is the same difference in the mode of administration. The machinery of a revolving light is never allowed to be out of order a single hour; the lamp must never go out until the sun rises to eclipse it; but a 'lock-up' is sometimes so mismanaged that prisoners suffer unto death, and the lamp of paupers' lives sometimes goes out from suffocation in alms-houses.

These are extreme cases, it is true, but they are not imaginary ones. It is manifest to all familiar with the working of public eleemosynary institutions, that many of them are managed upon a system of beggarly economy, which would be scouted as short-sighted and foolish in banks, railroad offices, manufactories, and the like.

But it is not parsimony in salaries of persons employed, and in the general administration of public eleemosynary institutions that does harm, so much as it is this parsimony manifested in the very conception of the plan of the institutions, and in the general principles of their organization.

Insanity takes its victims from the families of the rich and powerful as well as of the poor and weak, and therefore establishments for their care and cure are endowed with a munificence, and administered with a liberality which are unknown in most other public charitable institutions. They will not, however, be long unknown. Man is ever progressive. What of good he has been led to do by a lower motive, he will continue to do from a higher one. There will be a change in the mode of viewing and discharging the duties of what is now called public charity. A more enlightened public conscience will surely pronounce *some* of the present modes upon which we now so much plume ourselves, and which we think prove us particularly humane and Christian, to be only ingenious attempts to serve God and Mammon at the same time; for we huddle together in crowds some of the subjects of our public institutions, in spite of the plain principle that such close congregation is unwise and evil, and good only because it is cheap.

If we consider the principle and administration even of orphan asylums, which certainly have been, and still are blessed establishments, we shall see that they cannot do justice to their inmates; for has not each fatherless and motherless girl a claim, upon Christian principles, to the comforts and joys of such a home, and to such a share of woman's sanctifying nurture and love, as we give our own children, and such, as dying, we should wish to secure for them? Now is it not clear, that this claim cannot be satisfied when we put the orphan girl away from ourselves, into an establishment with a hundred others, where she can have those blessed influences in homœopathic doses only?

In the foundling hospitals of Southern Europe, we are shocked by the 'lean and hungry looks' of the infants, two or three, and sometimes even four of whom, depend upon one nurse for their nourishment. The poor little things 'peak and pine,' and moan. They struggle on for life a little while, contending for the breast; but only the most robust, or the one favored by the nurse, can hold out through infancy. The mortality among them would almost satisfy Herod's edict, without any sword. Such stint of bodily sustenance would not be tolerated in higher communities, and would be deemed barbarous in our own. But do we not stint and dwarf the souls and affections of little orphans by doling out the hundredth part of woman's love and nurture, and the hundredth part of the joys of home, when they need at least the tenth? And if it be so with the best of our eleemosynary institutions, and those managed by the best people, how must it be with others, — especially how must it be with the worst?

It is painful to dwell upon the objectionable features of establish ments so fair in front and in purpose, and which, in spite of all, do really effect much good; but it is only by correcting evils that we approach perfection.

Our public charitable and penal institutions — I mean those of the United States — are happily free from most of the grosser evils and abuses of some European ones, but not from all. Some Institutions raise their granite fronts upon the highway, and, like the Sphinx, charm us by the beauty of their humane face and lineaments, but, like that fabled monster, they have behind and within uncomely and inhuman parts.

It will be an easy matter for you, Gentlemen, to avoid the material errors, those I mean that concern material things, into which similar commissions have fallen; and I doubt not that you will. But you have a higher and more important duty, or you may construct your Commission so as to embrace one, and that is, to point out the principle on which the Institution shall be founded.

This is not the place to consider the comparative value of the separate and the congregate system of prison discipline, because for these girls there should be no prison, no semblance even of a prison, and no systematic and forcible confinement.

Since, however, one purpose of this letter is to urge the importance of the principle of separation, it may be not amiss to remark that the value of that principle in penal establishments is not duly recognized in our community, because it has never been brought fairly before the public here, as it has been elsewhere. This is unfortunate, because a full appreciation of the value of the principle which underlies this system, would be of great importance in determining the mode to be adopted in the reformation of girls.

It is indeed doubly unfortunate, because there is not only lack of knowledge, but erroneous ideas upon the subject prevail, and error is always worse than ignorance.

Some suppose that full consideration must have been given to this matter by the Prison Discipline Society which has so long existed among us, and by its journal; but if they consult the records of the Society, and the pages of the journal, they will find it is not so. The demerits and the failures of the Separate System have been carefully and elaborately set forth as they occurred in certain prisons, but not its successes and its merits. On the contrary, the Society early pledged itself to the support of another system by an express vote, and its journal carried out the pledge in a partisan spirit.

It was to bring the Society back to its proper impartial ground, and to obtain for the friends of the Separate System a fair hearing, that several members protested against the course that had been followed, and called for a change. This call was resisted, but being persevered in, it led to a public discussion several years ago, which will be remembered by those interested in such matters.

The protesters there were not the pledged advocates of the

Separate System, but were desirous of having a full and fair discussion of its merits as well as of its demerits. They insisted that the Society's journal should no longer be used as a lantern with an opening only on one side to show the merits of the Congregate System, but shrouding in darkness all the merits of the other. They persevered so long as there was any hope of putting the Society upon what they considered the proper and impartial ground, and then, sorrowful for the illiberality and ill temper with which they had been encountered, and for the heat which had been engendered by their perseverance in their right, despairing moreover of effecting any good through the Society, and pressed by other duties, they left it.

Others suppose the subject to have been duly discussed in print, and that a large pamphlet* which appeared soon after this public discussion was a *settler*, because no one replied to it. They, too, are greatly mistaken. Had there been any hope of obtaining a fair hearing, or any hope commensurate with the sacrifice of time and labor, it would have been easy to show that that able pamphlet, besides being grossly unfair to opponents, evaded the great principle, and raised a side issue about the comparative merits of particular prisons.

That pamphlet was industriously distributed in England, where as well as on the continent, the ablest minds were then earnestly engaged in studying matters of prison discipline, and where every thing really touching its great principles was eagerly sought for; but there it fell like a bullet of dough. There after numerous and patient experiments in general and local prisons; after earnest consideration by theoretical men and practical men; after long discussion by the press and by the Parliament, the government deliberately and finally adopted the principle which had failed even to find a fair hearing with us. And now, in that great land of common sense, entire separation for a considerable period, is a cardinal maxim in prison discipline, and convicts must be cut off even from the sight of each other, during the first year at least, of their imprisonment.

Now without advocating, and without ever having advocated the

* By the Hon. F. C. Gray.

introduction of what is called the Separate System, as heretofore practised in Philadelphia, Pentonville, or elsewhere, into our prisons for adults, I deeply regret that the importance of the principle of entire separation of persons convicted of offences, during a considerable period of their confinement, has not had due consideration here, because it is peculiarly applicable to the treatment of girls whom we would reform.

The plan advocated in the following letter to the Commissioners would require the entire separation of the girls from each other, because it would place them far apart. They would be widely distributed over the State, and though under the supervision of the Institution, yet under the immediate care of various families. By this plan we may take advantage of a law of human nature, which has not, to my knowledge, ever had definite consideration in schemes of reform. Whenever, in the course of human development, certain moral evils appear as the necessary consequences of a transition state of society, certain moral correctives also are sure to be developed. As in the aberration of a heavenly body, some hitherto latent force is certainly developed in time to prevent it from whirling into chaos, so in the wide deviations of man from the direct line of progress towards good, certain latent checks and balances suddenly appear and prevent the race from rushing to perdition. God sows good seed more widely than the devil can sow tares. The congregation of men in great cities, and other necessary phases of civilization, uniformly and certainly engender a class which is aptly called the criminal or dangerous class. This class multiplies rapidly, and seems to threaten property and morality, but at the same time the same causes develop certain moral agencies to counteract the evil. Among these agencies is the appearance of men and women who are natural born reformers; —who are fitted by their very organization, to save children from rushing to perdition, [illegible]

Now it is a remarkable fact, that choice spirits of this rare class are seldom found at the head of regularly organized establishments of reform. This is partly because the offices in such establishments are as likely to be filled by men who want the places as by men whom the places want, and partly because the natural reformers are not apt to come forth at any call except when pressing emergencies arouse them. If the child is overboard in their sight they rush in. From good Tata* Giovanni the Roman mason, to John Pounds the London hoemaker, it has always been the same. They have as much genius for improving children as Fulton or Whitney had for improving machinery; and their genius is as much higher as human souls are higher than steam engines and cotton gins. But they have the waywardness of genius too, and often mistake self-will for inspiration.

Roman John, while wielding the trowel, or English John the hammer, espies a ragged urchin prowling around with furtive glances, seeking what he may steal. Instead of crying 'Stop thief,' or calling the police, John says 'Come here, my little dear, and eat a crust of my bread.' The urchin, attracted by the friendly look and voice, comes readily, and with the bread gets kind counsel. He comes again as much for the counsel as for the bread. He loves to tell his story to John, because John loves to hear it. Love is the attraction that draws them together. John sorrows for the boy's crimes, and makes him sorrow also; but he so mingles love with reproof that the urchin will not go away; therefore at night John gives him a rug to lie down upon, and teaches him to say his prayers before he goes to sleep. In a few days the orphaned outcast has found a father and a friend whom he strives to imitate and to please, and he is satisfied; but John is not satisfied, because he has found a new want which craves new gratification. He seeks other little prowlers, therefore, brings them home, and feeds, lodges, and teaches them, hammering all the while for bread, until his mean little house is full of reformed Ishmaelites to whom he is a Father and Saviour, and for the love of whom they love virtue and eschew wickedness.

By-and-by John attracts or seeks notice, and gets means to leave off trowelling or hammering, and devote himself to reform, and his house becomes an institution. But, probably, he is soon interfered with by his patrons; he is trammelled by rules which are not half so good as his instincts; and the regular institution is less efficient than his irregular school was.

Or John dies, and with him dies the spirit of the place; and henceforth there is only dull routine; and things are done by cold formulas which should be done by earnest zeal and love. This was

* Tata, the familiar for *padre*, as Daddy for Father.

the fate of Tata Giovanni's establishment, though it is now under the protection of the Pope, and the direction of priests; and such has been the fate of others in Protestant countries.

It will be well if the strong and brave spirit of Nash, which has led him for so many years to share his room and crust with young thieves of London, whom his love attracted about him, and whom he won to virtue and confirmed in good habits until he could safely place them out as apprentices, or send them out as emigrants, — it will be well if his spirit, too, be not cramped in some way, now that his enterprise is taken under the patronage of the rich and great.

Those familiar with the history of establishments for reformation will recall many such instances. A man of natural fitness for the work gathers about him in *one small family*, youth of peculiar temper and disposition, called stubborn, perverse, or bad boys, whom others cannot manage, and they soon become gentle and docile under his plastic hands. His success attracts the attention of kind people, and his little private establishment receiving patronage, soon becomes a large and public one. But, generally, as it increases in size, it decreases in efficiency. The influence of the master-spirit, being counteracted or at least diluted by other influences, is less pervading; the one-man power is gone; the man himself soon goes with it, and in a few years the establishment falls into the hands of those who conduct it according to approved rules, and effect comparatively little good. One of the reasons for this has been mentioned above, to wit, the difficulty of finding a man ready made and fitted to fill a place, the peculiarities of which grew from the peculiarities of another man. But besides, there are the necessary dilution and diminution of the reformer's influence over his children, by reason of their great numbers. He could know intimately the character of five, ten, or even a score of children, and mark from hour to hour their changing condition and wants; he could hold so many near his heart, and make them *each* feel the close embrace; he could give to each what every child yearns for and needs, — parental love directed specially toward himself as an individual, — and in return for which, he will give up even the customary gratification of ill regulated desires. But when there come to be one, two, or three hundred, it is another matter. We should claim for the reformer too much of a divine attribute if we expected that he could know the crowd as he knows the individual, and too much of a yet diviner attribute, if we expected that he would love the multitude as a father loveth his only child. Henceforth he must regard and govern them as masses; whereas, they want to be loved and led as individuals; and it is only by being so loved and led, that they will give themselves up entirely to their leader.

Now the reformers, the Giovannis, the Nashes, the Vicherns, and their like, are only distinguished individuals of a numerous class. Nature intensifies in them certain mental and moral qualities to make types of the class; but they do not exhaust her. Thousands of men and women possess these same qualities, only in a lower degree. They do not feel the inspiring influence so strongly as to be forced to go and seek the work, but, if it is brought near them, they will naturally and eagerly take to it. They will not build up reform schools, but if a reforming influence is called for where they are, they will be the first to exert it. Such men and women are to be found in every town, and every circle; and if the unfortunate girls whose reformation you are to attempt should be placed in their neighborhood, they would seek them out. In this way you may take advantage of the natural arrangement above alluded to, more than you possibly can by building up a great reform school in one place.

It may be thought that the principle which I earnestly recommend will be adopted as a matter of course, and that it is already adopted in the Reform School at Westborough, because it is part of the system to apprentice the boys out after a certain time.

But there will be the greatest difference between having the separation of the children from each other and their apprenticeship in families, mere subordinate features of a system, and having them regarded as its great cardinal principles.

There will be the greatest difference between regarding a large central establishment, in which girls must be congregated and kept together awhile before apprenticeship, as a necessary and a desirable feature in the plan of reform, and regarding such an establishment as I do, to be unnecessary and most undesirable.

In my letter to the former Commission it was suggested, that by the plan proposed, the only building required would be a hired house for the Superintendent and his family, in which he could receive the girls from the Court, and keep them a few days until places were found for them. This house might be a very small one, if the immediate apprenticeship were the sole instrumentality of the Institution.

It may be said that this would inevitably cause confusion, because places could not be found fast enough to supply the demand. But this will not be so if we reverse the custom, and seek dear places for the children instead of cheap ones. Instead of apprenticing girls to those who will board and clothe them in consideration of the profit of their work, let the Institution seek a better class of families, by offering to keep the girls clad tidily at its own expense, and to pay from fifty to a hundred dollars a year, provided they received proper care and nurture; and such families would surely be found. If persons with children should be afraid to receive the girls, there are childless persons enough who would not be. The expense would not greatly exceed that of building up and supporting a great central establishment; but if it would cost more, that is no matter, provided the work of reformation were more effectually done; and that it could be done more effectually, and, in a greater proportion of cases, by an establishment such as I have alluded to, than by a great reform school on the plan of the Westborough School, I have no manner of doubt. That the system would be free from the serious and inseparable evils connected with a large congregation of girls of this class, seems quite certain.

I will not, however, prolong these desultory remarks, but close by beseeching you to consider well, whether the principle of your establishment shall be that of congregation or of separation; for upon this, more than upon any thing else, will depend the success of this most interesting undertaking. I beseech you to consider, that without any great pile of bricks and mortar, without any peculiar building at all, without any public noise or parade, without having any of these unfortunate and misguided girls exposed to the public gaze, or ever brought face to face with each other, you may organize a great reformatory Institution, numbering its pupils by hundreds, and extending its blessed influences far and wide throughout the State.

It was my purpose to describe and recommend such an Institution in the letter to a former Commission, which I now submit to you, with the assurance that I am aware of its crudity, and regret my inability to elaborate and complete it as the importance of the subject demands.

With great respect, faithfully yours,

S. G. HOWE.

BOSTON, Dec. 25, 1850.

HON. WM. APPLETON,

DEAR SIR, — Your letter of inquiry, respecting the best and most efficient method of conducting Reform Schools for Girls in Europe, did not reach me until I had returned to this country. My health did not allow me, while abroad, to renew my visit to charitable institutions, and I cannot, therefore, give you any 'facts and statistics' of recent date: but, as you do me the honor to consult me upon a most important subject, I venture to give you some thoughts upon it.

There are other things to be considered besides facts and statistics in planning an establishment of this kind. There are certain general principles which should underlie all reformatory establishments, like foundation stones, and without which they cannot be useful or lasting.

I have no faith in the reformatory machinery of penal establishments, for adults, when it is brought to bear upon the subjects *in masses;* and I have very little faith in such establishments for the reformation of youth. It is hard work to make straight a single crooked stick — harder yet, a bundle of them, *if taken together.*

Some observation and reflection have led me to question the soundness of the principles upon which most of the public establishments for the reformation of youth in Europe and this country are founded; and to think that they do much harm to some of their subjects, while doing some good to others. Such establishments may be considered as social evils; in some cases necessary evils, in others, 'unnecessary evils.' These terms are vague, but no matter if the meaning is clear. It is an evil to hang a criminal, or shut him up in prison for life; but it may, under certain circumstances, be a necessary one. It is an evil to shut up youth in houses of detention; and whether it be a necessary evil or not, depends upon whether the desirable ends, to wit, the reformation of those who are capable of reformation, and the safety of the community, can be secured in any other way or not; if they can, then such establishments are unnecessary evils.

You say, that our good Legislature had in view the 'State Reform School for Boys,' when they contemplated a Reform School for Girls. Let us enter into some general considerations which should be taken into account before founding a new Reform School, not forgetting, moreover, that what may do for boys is not necessarily well adapted for girls.

Some youths have the moral sentiments so deeply implanted in them by nature, that in whatever circumstances they may be placed, they will finally grow up to be virtuous and good persons. As some men, whom we call men of talent or genius, have by nature such strength and activity of intellect that nothing can prevent them from attaining intellectual eminence, so others have by nature such strength and activity of the moral sentiments, that nothing can prevent them from attaining moral eminence. Such men are not only 'a law unto themselves,' but a law unto others; for, as the man of high intellect exercises a great influence upon others, as he *radiates* light and knowledge around him, so the man of high moral nature exercises a great moral influence upon others. He diffuses morality and goodness around him. Virtue flows out at the touch of his garment. The highest men of this class, the types, have been so rare in ages past, or so few of them were known, that they shone out of the surrounding darkness like stars. They are becoming more common as the race becomes more elevated, and their individual influence is less extensive. Of this class, houses of reformation will have very few or none.

Other youths are so unfavorably constituted by nature, and have such innate activity of the lower propensities, with such feebleness of the moral sentiments, that, in whatever circumstances they may be placed, they will grow up to be vicious and depraved men. The curse seems to be upon them. The sins of their fathers are visited upon their heads. Their vicious tendencies are too strong to be suppressed, at least while young. They cannot be tamed more than can the untamable brutes. Now such persons exercise, involuntarily, perhaps, a most unfavorable influence upon others. They *radiate* and diffuse vice and evil around them, and none but souls of ethereal temper, — none but those who are a law unto themselves, can live uninjured in their baleful atmosphere. This class is much larger than the other, though it is growing smaller; but, unfortunately, it furnishes a considerable number of subjects for houses of reformation.

Youths of a third class are much more numerous, for the two classes of persons, just mentioned, whose natures are so strongly marked by good or evil, who diffuse around them virtue or vice, are few compared with the whole people. By far the greatest number are born without any strong and decided tendency to virtue or vice. They are the creatures of circumstances, and grow up to be virtuous or vicious according to the outward influences exercised upon them. They are furnished by nature with the raw material of character, and education gives it shape; for education forms only the *common*, not the *uncommon* mind. That this general classification is correct, is proved by the fact that 'criminals,' especially 'juvenile offenders,' come from that class of society most exposed to want and most exposed to temptation. The exceptions prove the rule. Out of this third great class, those, namely, without any strong natural bias to good or evil, the subjects for Houses of Reformation will be mostly drawn.

It is admitted on all hands that there are in Massachusetts several hundred girls, of tender age, and innocent as yet of any crime, who are surely doomed by surrounding evil influences to become the saddest specimens of humanity that the world exhibits, — vicious and depraved women in the bosom of an enlightened and virtuous community. Few, if any, of these, are of the first class mentioned above, or those who are a law unto themselves. A few belong to the second class, and they are of such low and vicious organization that it is hardly possible to change them. They *will* give themselves up to the dominion of animal passions, so long as those passions are stimulated by the hot blood of youth; and probably will continue in their indulgence long afterwards, by the force of habit. The great majority, however, are of the third class, or those who, if bred up in virtuous families, and under virtuous influences, will become virtuous; but if not, then vicious. They are now surrounded by vicious influences, and will fall a prey to bad men, if not saved by the good; and it is just as much a duty to save them, as if they were struggling in the waves before our eyes and calling upon us to throw them a plank.

It is certainly right and proper that the State should come to their aid. Nay, it is an urgent duty to do so. The only question is, how best to effect the object. It is now proposed to do so by gathering them together into one great establishment, and attempting to teach and train them there until they shall be so far reformed, as to be fit to be restored to society outside.

There are certain apparent advantages in this plan, and these have been so frequently and strongly set forth, that they need no consideration here. Let us see, however, if there be not grave objections to it, and whether we cannot have all the advantages in some other way, without the disadvantages.

I consider it to be certain that all establishments, in which a large number of persons of one sex live long together, are unnatural, unfavorable to the growth of social virtues and graces, and injurious to the moral nature in a greater or less degree. I would have this borne in mind as a cardinal maxim while reading what follows.

The degree in which they are injurious to the inmates, depends of course upon the extent to which the practice of congregating them together and isolating them from the world, is carried; but there is no escape from certain evil consequences. Nunneries, monasteries, armies, navies, boarding-schools, in short, every establishment of the kind, if its secret history were known, would probably show this. What we do know sufficiently confirms the *à priori* inference to warrant this conclusion.

Congregations of *young* persons of one sex are even more injurious than those of older persons. The young need the constant presence, the influence and the example of their elders. Nature mingles them in due proportion in common families and in general society, and any wide departure from this proportion, is unfavorable to the best moral growth.

But most especially undesirable, and as it seems to me, most especially unwise and hazardous, would be a congregation in one great household of young girls, in all, or in the majority of whom, bad habits have developed ill regulated desires. Such an establishment should never be thought of but as a matter of stern necessity.

Common sense points out that the principle upon which such cases should be treated is that of *separation* and *diffusion*, not *congregation* and *concentration*.

VICIOUSLY DISPOSED YOUTH SHOULD NOT BE BROUGHT TOGETHER, BUT PUT FAR ASUNDER.

Besides these considerations arising out of general principles, there are many and strong objections of a practical kind, to a great Reform School, in which several hundred girls should be congregated and made to live together. One of these is, that they *must be publicly exhibited;* they must become known to a large number of persons as belonging to a vicious class; they will get a character as such, and *it will stick to them through life!*

There is no way of avoiding this publicity, and its consequences, in a large establishment. The genius of our country, and the inquisitiveness of our countrymen demand it, and must have it; and they ought to have it, for it is a security against abuse.

The establishment should and would necessarily be inspected very frequently by a variety of officials, from governors to constables. Unofficial visitors, too, would find access in great numbers. The girls would become known to a large number of persons. They would find that they were considered as a class apart — as an unfortunate, if not a criminal class. But more and worse than all this — they would *learn to consider themselves as such!*

Think of the effect upon a timid and sensitive girl, (for we must think most of those who are most likely to be reformed,) of a few years passed in such a situation, and say whether some of the effects must not necessarily be injurious.

I have now in my mind one or two worthy women, who were, when young girls, inmates of a House of Reformation. They may be aware that it was the means of saving them from sin, but I know that they consider it a sore misfortune, that the name 'House of Reformation Girls,' clings to them through life, and diminishes their chance for usefulness and happiness.

If it is granted that the classification made above be correct, and that the great majority of youth in Houses of Reformation be of that great class of *common* minds whose character is formed by circumstances, it may seem strange that so few are reformed in those institutions, and is avowedly the case. Ninety-five out of a hundred might be reformed, and they would be reformed, if placed in the most favorable circumstances. But there are many drawbacks to the usefulness of such establishments. There is much evil mixed with the good they do. The work is up-hill work, and done under great disadvantages. Now all these unfavorable circumstances, and still many others, would prevail in a great establishment for girls, and impede the work of their reformation.

If the Master of a House of Reformation, and his family, supposing them to be fitted by nature and education for their high duty, could take each boy separately, and keep him under their control and influence for a few years, they would be almost certain to reform ninety-five out of every hundred. They would cut their pupil off from all evil associations; they would surround him with kind and virtuous influences; they would win him by love and virtuous example; they would correct those very passions, — love of imitation, and love of approbation, the abuse of which had led to his evil course, into instruments for his reformation; and they would certainly reform him, unless he were one of the class I have referred to, who by their very organization are incorrigible, who are not morally responsible, who are moral idiots, and to be treated as such. The success would be much more certain with girls, (if they had not been absolutely ruined,) for though they are *less likely* than boys to be benefited by residence in a public House of Reformation, they are *more likely* to be benefited by the virtuous influences of a private family.

Now, why cannot a master of a House of Reformation reform a like proportion in a large establishment? Because he has not the advantages of the principle of *separation* and *diffusion*, but, on the contrary, he has the disadvantage of the *concentration* of the vicious material; because there will be a few of the incorrigible class among his boys, and they will diffuse around them their vicious influence; and because, at first, and for a long time, perhaps always, the *public opinion of the community is against him.* He and his family and his assistants are but a dozen virtuous persons surrounded by three or four hundred viciously disposed youth; the moral atmosphere is a bad one; the sympathies of the *majority* are with the evil doers and evil thinkers, and he is obliged to maintain his authority by physical force and restraint. These could not be given up safely in any of our Houses of Reformation, even for a day. Now physical force and restraint do not effect moral reformation; but, on the contrary, they are almost certain to impede it. If it were not that the master calls in to his aid, and enlists upon his side, those few among his boys in whom the moral sentiments are by nature rather strong, — who are more disposed to virtue than vice, he would be overcome in the contest. *Outward* order and decorum might prevail in his establishment, but it would be a moral pandemonium.

I think that most masters of Houses of Reformation will admit that without the aid and assistance, and the moral influnence of this class of boys, they could do but little.

I think, too, it will be found that the most striking cases of reformation in such houses, are boys of the first class mentioned above, but never those of the second, or the naturally bad. But the most numerous cases are those of the third class, who were made vicious by extraordinary pressure of vicious influence. They are favorably organized for receiving and retaining either good or bad impressions; they would have been reformed quite as easily, if not more so, out of the House, by a little aid and assistance from some kind friends, and some of them perhaps would have saved themselves by their own efforts.

It must have struck careful observers of Houses of Reformation for juvenile offenders, that there are usually a certain number of *show pupils*, who are considered as remarkable instances of the power of reformation; who obtain and deserve certain privileges; who are employed and trusted, and who promise fairly to make good men. Such boys will be found to be naturally well organized, kindly disposed, docile, and full of love of approbation; they are boys who are more easily made good than bad.

Now, notwithstanding the aid and assistance of such superior spirits, the masters have to *enforce* order; that is, they have to depend upon bars and bolts, and a reserved force, which may or not be used; and they have little opportunity of giving their boys what they most need — *moral training*. This is a great and serious objection. The young need not only teaching and preaching, not merely instruction and precept, but they need even more than these, good example and opportunity of imitating it. They need to *exercise* their moral powers, to struggle with temptation and overcome it, rather than to be removed from it; in a word, they need moral gymnastics, moral training, and without that, prayers and precepts, tracts and sermons, avail but little.

The show pupils mentioned above, get something of this training;

they are trusted; they have liberty of action; they meet and overcome temptation, and are stronger for every victory; but the boys of weaker moral sentiment, the *bad* boys, as they are called, they who most need moral gymnastics, and who most need the practice of resisting temptation, have less opportunity of doing so, if indeed they have any.

It is related of Captain Maconochie, formerly Governor of Norfolk Island, a man of most humane and beautiful spirit, and one of the most successful practical managers of convicts, that he used in particular cases to train men to resist the temptation to drink by putting the dram before them, while he surrounded them with moral inducements to refrain from touching it. A convict who had brandy in his cell, and yet could keep the bottle imp safe under the cork all night long, would be safer than one who had merely pledged himself never to yield to a future temptation. However extravagant this instance may appear, the principle is the true one. It is indeed the one upon which nature proceeds in the moral world.

I remember that a former Superintendent of the House of Reformation in this city, used to send a certain class of boys whom he could trust, into the city, to the post-office, and upon various errands, and even upon furloughs, as a reward of merit. It was objected to by some, on account of the risk, and on account of doubt, whether, as the House was a penal establishment, and a place of detention, it was right to lose sight of the prisoners. The effects however were certainly good. I used to think, when I saw a boy going away from this 'lock-up-house,' and into the very neighborhood of his old haunts and old companions, that he was going to have a struggle with the devil, and when I saw him come back of his own accord at the end of his furlough, I knew he had beaten him.

This is *training;* this is what all the boys need; but, organized as Houses of Reformation are in this country, the great majority of inmates, *those especially who most need it*, cannot get it. It is not the good boys, — the show pupils, who most need reformation, it is the bad ones. They that be whole need not a physician, but they that are sick.

In some of the European establishments for reformation of vicious youth, this principle is acted upon more than in ours, indeed it is fundamental, especially at Mettray in France. But that establishment is conducted upon entirely different, and, as I think, upon better principles. There is no great House of Detention as with us; no bars or bolts; not even a high wall around the premises. The boys may run away if they choose; but though they are restrained only by moral force, they do not do so. This is not the place, however, to go into a description of that beneficent establishment; to raise questions about the soundness of some of the principles upon which American Houses of Reformation are managed; or to inquire whether more good could not be effected by less expenditure of time and money in a different manner, — any farther than such questions and inquiries may be useful in the consideration of the best means of reforming girls. Even for this purpose it is an unwelcome task, because it may seem derogating from the high character already enjoyed by our own State Reform School, which is already counted among the jewels of the Commonwealth by so many persons, in confident anticipation of the good it is destined to do.

All honor to the noble and generous founder of that establishment, and to the many good men who have labored, and are laboring, to make the seed which he planted and watered in his lifetime, bear great harvest of good after his death. It is to be wished that they had an establishment less objectionable in the principles upon which it is organized, and less liable to neglect or abuse in its administration. But, leaving that, let us see whether a greater amount of good cannot be done to the unfortunate girls of our Commonwealth by a less complicated and expensive machinery, and by means better adapted to their peculiar situation and wants.

Suppose that there are at this moment three hundred unfortunate girls, some of them as yet innocent of any grave crime, but all in instant and deadly peril; who are about to make fearful shipwreck of their temporal and spiritual welfare; who have no hope of salvation but in some public effort to be made in their behalf by the State; how shall Massachusetts save these, her perishing daughters? The cry is, Erect a State Reform School. But I say, Massachusetts has already many THOUSAND REFORM SCHOOLS built up by God himself, and spread broadcast over her hills and valleys, better in all respects than any that the wit of man can devise, for reforming vicious inclinations and implanting good ones. She has more than fifty thousand virtuous and intelligent families; and let us see if among them there are not enough who could be persuaded to take charge of these unfortunate girls, and reform them. If we can do so, we may be sure that we shall do a wise, an effectual, and a blessed work, blessed to all parties, the reformer as well as the reformed.

It seems to me that we have the elements with which to work ready to our hands; that there is virtue enough among us to leaven this little lump of vice; and that instead of gathering these unfortunate girls together, from all parts of the Commonwealth, and shutting them in one great congregation of sinners, society should take them to its bosom, and attempt to win them back to virtue.

I think a plan can be pointed out, by which, taking advantage of the *natural reform schools* existing in the Commonwealth, a fair trial of the capacity of the girls for reformation may be made, without the outlay of such a vast capital as will be necessary for the proposed great central establishment; a plan too, which, while it holds out great promise of success, cannot occasion great loss or harm by its failure.

Facts and experience, though ever so homely, are what the good people of Massachusetts value more than theories and speculations, though ever so fair; let me hold out a fact then, as a sort of lure to make them attend a little to what may be said afterwards in way of theory. When I was a Director in the House of Reformation in Boston, it used to be the practice to keep the boys a long time, many years even, in the House, and then apprentice them out to mechanics, farmers and others. At first, these persons were required to obligate themselves to fit out the lad with a suit of clothes on his becoming of age, and to give him a sum of money.

I think there was a great fundamental error in the principle upon which the establishment was managed — that of trusting too much to the machinery of reformation in the House, and of keeping the boys a long time under its operation, until it was supposed they had become fit for apprentices. But the important fact to be noted is, that some of the most satisfactory cases of reformation that I knew, were those effected out of the House, and in families, after the machinery of the Institution had failed to do them any good. They were incorrigible while in it.

But besides these cases occurring in public establishments, every person who has had much practical knowledge of society, can recall cases of wayward and apparently vicious youth who have been reformed by kind and wise treatment, and by being thrown into a circle of virtuous acquaintances, especially by being brought under the saving influence of the society of virtuous women.

Proceeding, then, upon the principle above alluded to, and encouraged by the facts mentioned, I would propose that an institution for the reform of girls be upon the following plan.

Suppose we are to begin with one hundred girls, who are not to be admitted all at once, but at first about twelve each month. Let us find an intelligent, benevolent, active and practical man, who has a wife of the like character, and let them be appointed Superintendent, and Matron, with liberal salaries. Give them ample power and discretion. Let them select and nominate their assistants, who of course would be women, and such noble specimen of womankind as Massachusetts yields, — her richest produce. Make the Superintendent responsible to a Board for the general *result*, but not for his daily doings; let him be the *head* and not the servant of the establishment; tell him what he is to do, and let him do it in his own way; if he cannot do it well, exchange him for one who can.

Let there be a common house hired and furnished for him; or a contract made with some good family, to board him and his officers, and as many girls (not over twelve years of age) as may be sent to him. They should, however, be sent a few at a time, at first, and only as fast as he gives notice of his readiness, so that he might not have many at a time upon his hands. These arrangements made, the Institution would be ready to go into operation. It might commence indeed in one month after the passage of the act creating it.

The first business of the Superintendent would be to procure places in suitable families for the girls as fast as they should be sent to him. He would not, however, follow the old plan; he would not count upon people paying for keeping the girls as domestics; or taking them in the expectation of grinding as much work out of them as possible; — on the contrary, he would offer *to pay the families for taking them!* He would issue a stirring circular, setting forth the necessity of the case, and calling on the women of the Commonwealth, to come to his aid in the attempt to save these perishing girls.

To any respectable and suitable family, that would take one of them, bring her up properly for two, three, or more years, give her instruction in needle-work and house-work, and teach her at home, or send her to town school in winter, he would offer not only the advantage of her services as a domestic or an apprentice, but furnish her clothing, and guaranty to them the sum, say of fifty dollars a year, to be paid at the expiration of her time, provided they faithfully performed their duty to her.

As soon as a number of places was provided, the Superintendent would give notice of his readiness, and the magistrate would send the girls to Worcester, where they would be taken in charge by the Superintendent's wife, and watched over, studied and cared for. The Superintendent would get all possible information about each girl's case, her peculiarities and her wants. He would select the proper family from among his applicants and send her to them at once, under charge of one of his assistants. The assistant would perhaps tarry a little with the girl in her new home, to give and receive all necessary information, and then return to Worcester, to go out again upon the same errand. The hundred would be soon placed. The Institution would be in full operation, and yet there would be *no pupils to be seen.* The business of the assistants would then be, to go from place to place, each one in her circuit, and visit the girls as often, and tarry with them as long as might be necessary. They would learn from the families how the girl was behaving, and from the girl, how she was treated. Each case would be rigidly inspected, noted down, and the details sent to Worcester. There might be as many girls thus placed out, as there are boys in the State Reform School. They might be vigilantly watched and under constant control; the Institution might be in all respects, as powerful and as efficient as that is, and yet there would be no great building, no great congregation of girls, and no display. The machinery would be out of sight, but working silently and smoothly, and its influence be felt from Cape Cod to Berkshire. Besides its immediate officers, it would find every where earnest and able assistants in its work of love. It would not have to depend alone upon the family in which the girls were placed, but in every town would enlist one or more benevolent women, and thus secure sympathy and friendship for them.

Can one doubt that, with the authority of law, the aid of the

State, the countenance of the public, the labors of zealous and efficient assistants, the co-operation of families in which these girls were placed, and the support of several earnest and religious women in each town, a Superintendent could not reform more out of three hundred girls, than if he had them shut up altogether in one building with ever so efficient corps of officers about him?

Can any one whose creed is, and whose practice should be,— Do unto others as you would they should do to you,—can he hesitate which situation he would prefer, for his own perverse child, a residence in the bosom of a private family, or in a community of vicious girls, though ever so well regulated, where she would be exposed to public gaze, and necessarily get for life the name and character of a 'House of Reformation Girl?' Surely not!

Such is the general outline of an institution, which might perhaps meet the present wants, and answer the pressing call. Of course, there will be objections urged against it, some of which, may as well be met now. It will present advantages also, and in noticing these, it will be fair and proper to refer, by way of comparison, to the State Reform School for Boys.

The first objection which will occur to some, is the difficulty of finding proper places for the girls, and engaging proper persons to take the charge of them.

In order to overcome this difficulty, it will be necessary that some substantial advantage be held out to induce people to take them, and this will be found in the service of the girls as domestics, and the money to be paid at the end of their time of service. The sum of fifty dollars is named merely as approximative; it might be less, if it were found it would do to diminish it; or it might be increased, if it were found necessary. If it were put even as high as one hundred dollars, it would not equal the cost of the boys at the State Reform School, for we shall see afterwards, that their board alone cost the State thirty-four dollars a year.

Let it not be said that the motive held out is a low one, and that families which could be induced to receive these girls in consideration of the advantage to be obtained from their services as domestics, and by hope of the premium, are by that very fact unworthy of the charge. Men, and good men too, are impelled by various motives, some higher and some lower. Many people might be induced to co-operate in this blessed work of reforming girls, by hope of these advantages, who would not have touched it without them; but, who, nevertheless, could not be made to touch it by any temptation whatever, if it were not a good work. Again, be it not said that people who can be led to do what they would not otherwise do by considerations of personal interest, are unfit to bring up girls, lest we condemn our own fathers and mothers, and most of those who bring up the youth of our Commonwealth, — lest we condemn our ministers, our schoolmasters, and large classes of good men.

An earnest and eloquent Superintendent would overcome this difficulty. He would appeal to the moral and religious sense of the community, and his appeals would be answered by moral and religious *women* from the villages and hamlets of the country. The wives of small farmers, mechanics, indigent clergymen and schoolmasters, childless people especially, would offer their services to help him in his truly Christian work. It would indeed be a burning shame if in Massachusetts, where so many women can labor to convert the far-off heathen, or free the far-off bondmen, and can open their hearts and houses to fugitives from slavery, there should be none to convert their sisters from worse than heathenism, or rescue them from worse than servile bondage; and none to open their hearts and their houses to fugitives from greater monsters than slave owners. It would be wronging the noble women of Massachusetts to suppose that it is necessary to leave several hundred girls of tender age, to run to swift destruction, or to be shut up in a great prison-house because charity and love had gone abroad to do their work, and left only cold hearts and hearths at home. No! this difficulty, great as it is, could be overcome.

Another objection that may be urged is, that abuses may be committed, that the girls may be ill treated, and possibly their ruin accomplished. Well, there will be abuses; and so there will be every where. Hired servants are sometimes abused. Even in Houses of Reformation there are sometimes great abuses; and our own is far from being perfect. But under the plan now proposed, with the frequent visits of the regular assistants, with the watchfulness of friendly women, and with the account which the girls would themselves give, we should have, if not quite so much security against abuses as in a great

House of Detention, enough at least to induce us to run some small risk in view of the greater advantages of the plan in many other respects.

Still another objection may be urged, by men of little faith in virtue, on the score of danger in scattering the seeds of vice over the Commonwealth, and corrupting the virtuous families of the country. But the seeds of vice need vicious soil in which to take root; they perish in good soil, as seeds of goodness are apt to perish in bad soil. Besides, the virtue of our women is not made of sugar or salt, to be melted by the least exposure. If half a dozen good girls in the country are not more than a match for one evil-disposed girl from the city, — if they will not rather bring her over to them, than she bring them over to her, then there is not much to be said for the strength of their virtue, — that is all.

Besides, oh men of little faith and much conscientiousness, who stickle about the *right* of exposing virtue, suppose even that there be some small danger, and that in a few cases there would be harm done, — have these girls no *rights*, and ought we to shun all danger to ourselves, if by no other means than incurring it, we can make the most effectual effort to save them from perishing? If one of these poor girls were sinking in the waves, would you not, and should you not, peril your life to save hers? and now that more than her life is in danger, should you not risk something to save it?

Such are the principal objections, and such are the hasty replies to them; let us now look at some of the advantages of the plan here sketched, over that of a great Reform School, such as it is proposed to organize.

In the first place, even the advocates and admirers of Reform Schools for Boys, have their doubts about such establishments being well calculated for Girls. It would be easy, were there room in this short paper, to set forth several reasons for entertaining these doubts; and several considerations, drawn from the peculiarities of the female character, unfavorable to the plan of congregating girls of such character together. It would at least be a doubtful, and in some sense a dangerous experiment; but the plan above proposed, requires no investment of capital in lands and buildings; it is not one, which once entered upon must be continued for any time. If not found to answer, it can easily be abandoned without loss.

Another advantage of such an establishment over a great central school, would be its economy, though on this I would not lay much stress

Let us examine a little the expense of the State Reform School for Boys.

The capital already invested in land, buildings, &c., is about	$100,000
Annual interest on capital,	6,000
" cost of administering on the institution, salaries, wages, and support of officers,	7,250
" cost for fuel, light, and other current expenses,	3,200
" " of board for three hundred boys at thirty-four dollars,	10,200
	$26,650

These items, saving the first one, are taken from the Third Report of the Trustees, (page 7.) They make a deduction indeed, of $3,108 as the probable earnings from the labor of the boys during the year; but, it is safe to say, that, one year taken with another, the profits of their labor will not more than make good the wear and tear, and destruction of property, so that it is not safe to put down the annual cost of keeping these boys at less than $26,650. But the cost of each boy to the State, is not merely the three hundredth part of this sum, or $88, if the usual plan is pursued, and they remain several years in the house. The Trustees say in their Second Annual Report, (page 4,) 'The boys shall be sent here during their minority; that this was the intention of the framers of the law, and should be the rule of the administration.' It is plain, however, from other parts of their report, that they intend to apprentice out a portion at least of the boys. If we take two years only as the average time of their stay in the house, their cost *while there* will be $176; if three years, then it will be $264, and so on. It is to be feared that they will be obliged to hold out some other inducement than the services which the boys can render in order to get the right class of persons to take them; if they do, then the expenses of the establishment will be increased by so much; if they do not, then it may be that places may be found for girls likewise, without the premium proposed.

Let it not be supposed, from these remarks, that the expenses are considered too great. The institution seems to be managed with economy, and if the expenses were far greater, and yet necessary for the purpose of reformation, it should be paid freely. God forbid, that Massachusetts should count too closely the cost of any such work; that she should weigh money against her children's wants; or, doing so, that she should be so foolish as not to know which is worth most. Though the cost of each boy were a thousand dollars, yet, if when he becomes of age he is really reformed, he would be a cheap subject at that, for society would gain more than principal and interest of the money by having a productive member instead of a thief. Suppose these boys were captive to a savage enemy, who demanded a thousand dollars a head for their ransom, should we not pay it? And are they not captives to the great enemy of mankind?

But, though we would have the State go on and expend all that may be *necessary* for the reformation of boys, still, economy is ever to be kept in view; and if a feasible plan for the reformation of girls can be devised, which is much simpler and cheaper, this is, so far, a great advantage.

The plan proposed above would be exceedingly simple, and it would be very cheap compared with an establishment upon the model of the Boys' School.

The expenses can be reckoned upon one's fingers.

The salary of a Superintendent and his wife,	$2,500
" " " eight assistants,	2,000
Board of the above, and an average of six girls,	2,600
An ample allowance for travelling expenses and extras would be,	1,400
Total,	$8,500

Salaries should be put high, in order to secure high qualifications. There would be no other expenses, except the premium to be paid for each girl, at the expiration of her apprenticeship, and this, if put at fifty dollars, would be only equal to the expense of boarding a boy one year and a half at the State Reform School; whereas, in all probability, he will have to remain there much longer.

The economy, then, of this plan, would be most striking: there would be no need of a great outlay of capital; the interest upon this, and the loss by wear and tear, and destruction of property, would all be saved. It is easy to see, that an establishment of this kind could be carried on for much less than the cost of one upon the model of the present State Reform School.

Another advantage of this plan would be its simplicity. This will be plain to all who are familiar with the principles on which great institutions should be managed, and who are satisfied with obtaining results, though the means are ever so unostentatious. With some very charitable and well-meaning persons, this advantage will go for nothing; possibly it may make the plan less acceptable. They must see and feel the machinery, in order to believe in the effect. They must have things in the concrete, — in visible and tangible shape, in order to have faith in them. Many understand that water quickens the drooping corn, and thank God for the rushing rain, which falls noisily in their neighborhood, but heed not the gentle dew that comes quietly down, and broods over the broad earth all night long, refreshing and fertilizing it. With such persons, an institution, in order to obtain respect, must have a vast local habitation, and a great name. It must show its brick and mortar credentials. It must have a list of titled and distinguished persons as its patrons, and a display of officers actually working upon their materials before the public eye, as mechanics work at their trade while drawn in carts in public processions. Many would want to see the process of making bad girls into good, and to have a great central establishment in which to carry it on. With such, the plan set forth above would find no favor.

Another advantage of this plan, and surely not a small one, would be, that it might be managed almost entirely by women. A Superintendent has been named; but perhaps even his duties might be discharged by a Woman. The institution would differ from others of its kind, in that it would have but little outward material machinery. The power and influence would come from moral agency, and that could best be discharged by women. They could do the higher and more important parts of the work better than any man, and would need his services only for less important and merely mechanical affairs.

There would be a fitness and propriety in giving this work of reforming girls into the hands of women, and they would doubtless do it with a tact and ability that men could not imitate.

Another consideration in favor of this plan of placing these girls in good families, rather than congregating them all together, is, that society would seem to show a higher sense of duty, and a more tender regard for these its unfortunate children, by taking them, as it were, to its very bosom. We should in this way come more nearly up to the performance of a common duty, and in which all should partake, than by appointing deputies to do it. Thus to bring the work of reform before a multitude of persons, so that those who have a natural tact and capacity for it may engage in it, would be of great use to them, for happy is every one that findeth what his soul needeth. It would, moreover, be well for the girls, in so far as it would give greater chance for the development of affections and virtuous desires, by which means alone can evil thoughts and desires be effectually extinguished. They have, as we all have, sympathies and antipathies which can neither be accounted for nor overcome. Those beloved of all whom they meet, are rare in this world; rarer yet would be one who loves nobody; but rarest of all, one whom nobody could love. Many a poor girl, held to be stubborn and heartless, may be utterly unable to get within the sphere of attraction of any one of the half dozen worthy and skilful teachers in a House of Reformation. She cannot like them, try she never so hard, (though they cannot get any more satisfactory reason therefor than could Doctor Pell); nay, she may hold them in positive dislike without any known cause, and finally be set down as incapable of affection, and therefore incorrigible. But perhaps this very close-hearted and unloving girl may be irresistibly attracted by some congeniality of nature to some farmer's wife or daughter, or to some virtuous domestic, and pour out into her bosom the affections long pent up in her own.

It may be said that in so multiplying the opportunities for receiving good impressions, we shall be also multiplying those for receiving evil ones; but while by this plan of dispersion of the girls in the community, though still watching and restraining them, we multiply greatly the former, we do not multiply in anything like the same degree the latter, — for a girl shut up in a house with a hundred others, many of whom are corrupt, is continually exposed to evil influences.

I will not here anticipate any more objections that may be made to this mode of action in behalf of these unfortunate girls. Unfortunate they truly are; more so (if left to their probable fate) than the Blind, the Deaf, or even the Insane. Few, if any of them, can be considered responsible for the life they have led. Most of them are the victims of circumstances; indeed, it may be said, that, in one sense, they are the victims of society itself. Had they been taken from their cradles, and had they exchanged places with the infants of wealthy and refined families, they would now be objects of our admiration and love, while those who are now so loved and admired would perhaps be the outcasts. Let it be considered, that if they have not the graces and refinements which education would have brought out,—if fierce passions have been developed instead of gentle affections, it is more their misfortune than their fault.

Let society, then, consider carefully what is really the wisest and best plan for saving these girls, and let no considerations of economy, no selfish fears, no false shame, prevent it being carried out. By following this course, not only will the best chance be given them for growing up to be virtuous and intelligent women, but the most good will be done to all who engage in the work; for they who honestly attempt good deeds; they who earnestly aspire to generous ends, are sure to be the gainers, let the result be what it may. The blessing will come back to society twofold; for the bad will be made good; the good who labored to make them so, will become better.

There is this great satisfaction to be had, that whatever may be done, whatever plan may be adopted, the condition and prospect of these poor girls cannot fail to be improved. Massachusetts has heard the cry of her children, and will come speedily to their relief.

Very faithfully yours,

S. G. HOWE.

Hon. William Appleton.

www.ingramcontent.com/pod-product-compliance
Lightning Source LLC
LaVergne TN
LVHW011122110826
845150LV00008B/2219

* 9 7 8 1 4 1 8 1 9 5 4 2 7 *